Twenty-four Vocalises

For Alto, Baritone and Bass

Major Scales

H. Panofka. Op. 81, Book 1

Minor Scales

10

Agility

Agility

Triplets

20

Triplets

Groups of 2 Slurred Notes

Portamento

Portamento

Portamento

Portamento

38

Portamento

Andante leggiero

Twenty-four Vocalises

For Alto, Baritone and Bass

Dotted Notes

H. Panofka. Op. 81, Book II

Syncopation

Legato

Appoggiatura, Gruppetto, Turn and Inverted Mordent

* Also written

52

* Performed thus:

54

Preparatory Study for the Trill

Practise at first **Lento,** then **Moderato, Allegro** and **Allegro molto**

Agility

62

Trills

Arpeggios
Also practise staccato

Arpeggios
Also practise staccato

Chromatic Scales

Chromatic Scales

Intervals